John McAuliffe
SELECTED POEMS

John McAuliffe

SELECTED POEMS

WAKE FOREST UNIVERSITY PRESS

First North American edition

First published in Ireland in 2021 by

The Gallery Press and edited by Peter Fallon

© John McAuliffe, 2022

For permission, write to

Wake Forest University Press

Post Office Box 7333

Winston-Salem, NC 27109

WFUPRESS.WFU.EDU

ISBN 978-1-943667-04-8 (paperback)

LCCN 2022931554

Designed and typeset by

Nathan Moehlmann,

Goosepen Studio & Press

Cover Image: [detail] *Plums, Knife and Window*, 1949

William Scott, 1913–1989

© Estate of William Scott, 2022

National Museums Northern Ireland, Belfast

Ulster Museum Collection, BELUM.U2475

Publication of this book was made possible
by generous support from the Boyle Family Fund

Printed in Canada

Contents

OF ALL PLACES (2011)

THE WAY IN (2015)

THE KABUL OLYMPICS (2020)

for Nancy

John McAuliffe
SELECTED POEMS

A BETTER LIFE (2002)

A Change of Scenery

When first you moved in
you'd a view of the mountains
but after what seems a lifetime
the planted, salt-wind-torn firs
have screened both lawn and house;

now, at the exact sensible horizon,
you're perched on a ladder,
axe and saw your musical instruments,
leaning in to the task, cutting out
our view of the mountains.

The Long Weekend

We set out before dark,
but late, and right on time
to join the after work

traffic jams,
nothing for it but to wait
till they pull into homes

and clear the road at last.
We stop for nothing,
drive at our pool of light,

reach, by ten, the pier
and make our bright entrance
into the canal's nightworld,

which sleeves us in silence—
midges on the water,
fish biting ripples,

in the sedge a scatter
of mallards and their drake.
A swan circles

and settles in our wake,
a pheasant whirrs overhead,
we chug from lock

to lock, between unlit fields
that look white and out of character:
alone, for all the world,

we wave to each other
from the barge's
prow and tiller,

nothing between us,
such sweet exchange,
and time ticking over, urgent

as the rented, well-oiled engine.

The Crossroads

The streets are cruel to the chrome relic,
the gale blows, the thorns rust, his jaw drops,
the world and its mother, time, zoom
by his stone grotto like tanked-up joyriders.

He'd give his right side to set us straight,
to speak in the voice of our fathers
or take the fresh air as a pulpit;
as if it too were a matter of faith.

Weeds crack the tarmac, we slip by
into our snares and habits, turning on our lives
like ravenous and cornered animals
as if all we wanted was to be out of this world.

The Street

for John B. Keane

On the street, you wouldn't know what was just finishing,
swept clean already of dockets and tickets, the mingled smell gone
of cigars, straw, horses. Bird's lorries rumble out of town
past late Mass traffic, the odd mitching teenager and us, shopping
for the papers before we drive away home to Dublin. 12:15
and the whole clean town like a set that's just been deserted,
the loudspeakers broadcast Radio Kerry to no one.
A boy drizzles water into window boxes above the Archway,
a man puts a box accordion into the boot of his Datsun.

In Jet's the news is someone's stepped in front of the Cork train,
might the match be delayed? Nobody can say.
The L&N's shop assistant is glad the week is gone:
"Now, at last, things'll quieten down. But ye're off anyway"—
she measures our life like a basket of shopping.
And we make out the days ahead: school traffic, the rustle of shops,
the street's habitual walkers, the wash of rumor, the drift
of late-night talk of money made and lost, winter settling
in the street till it's black and white with rain and frost.

A Good Story

In the beginning was the conversation—the subject,
your home: square fields, five-bar wooden gates,
an even sloping greenness, groves of larch and oak
under which the animals rested or cropped at grass,
and all beneath a blue sky with a single tiny speck of cloud.

In the end it was a meadow whitening in starlight
and a road reduced to stones of every size,
potholes, dockleaves, encroaching bindweed,
bees, ragwort, a rustling ditch by the side,
a line of grass through the middle

tall and wild as your tales of the *Titanic*
and a seafaring gran-aunt, the Chinese whispers
about the year 1900 and a one-way ticket
to Saigon, or was it Ceylon, a good story about
a bottle of smoke, the lost land, a liter of vodka

that required your health—and a sigh, hushed,
like the air in this overgrown passage that leads
nowhere, for you are fragile as paper and your real estate
a stash of old currency and an expired blue passport
inky and true with stamped dates and trade routes.

Going Places

It doesn't happen often. Stuck in my room, say,
looking at rain or for a book, seeing that the floor may
need hoovering, hungover possibly,
rearranging the postcards on the wall:
                                        At times like this
I begin to remember childhood afternoons,
sitting in the back seats of cars, going places,
telephone wires on either side, like fences
for giant invisible horses.

Nightjar

Everyone knew about it before long,
my mother's mother's return
to Newmarket from Hong Kong
with her policeman, his pension

and, stranded with them, her ayah,
who with her eyes closed and no one about
would burn orange peel on the Aga
and kept one other personal habit,

hanging washed jars off the ash trees
in her family's back garden
where they'd outstare the neighbors
like some never-seen-before bird.

Africa

Heat rises, palpably, having scorched and cracked the earth.
In the distance, unreal as a cloud, a mountain looms;
a few kids amble by with shorts on and nothing else.
At night, at their watering holes, I listen to their fathers:
"If this weather doesn't break...," "It's like bloody Africa."

Missing

A yearling in a drained dyke,
a carthorse where the stream changed course,
a Shetland in a quarry in Kanturk,
a skull (unknown) beneath the floor

of the stepdancers' ruined house,
a goat's head that made the wind sound,
a king's ransom that was paid twice.
A rumor taking root underground.

Costello's Legend

from Douglas Hyde's Love Songs of Connacht

He heard too late
about Una's love.
He'd escaped south,
she was in her grave.

Afterwards he began
a life of adventure,
swam the Shannon at Glin,
saved towns from the invader,

tamed horses, wild boar,
slew champions in prize fights,
you had to be there
to credit his feats.

The First Round

The cars pulled up from 11 and the quiet backstreets packed out:
the visitors opened car doors and, at boots that stayed open,
they stood side by side to drink tea, then trailed off
towards town to talk down their chances and form.

Come mid-afternoon they were back wearing different colors
and I joined them streaming east to the park along the banks of the river.
For hours the cars were left unattended, the buses empty
that blocked up the sidestreets that no one wanted access to anyway.

If you couldn't go you were probably at home in front of the TV
or you'd no time for it and you'd your feet up reading the Sundays
or you were away at the beach where there was noise in the distance
and a radio broadcast the latest as your eldest aimed stones at the sea.

By nightfall there was no trace bar their papers snagged in the gutter.
Where once they'd catch trains or hitch lifts to go home for the cows
they hit town, shouting salutations and *The Fields of Athenry*
and bare-chested, cider-drinking teenagers hung flags off the statuary.

The late news called it shock, longshot, turn-up, reversal,
and the highlights missed the central event-changing incident.
At work, for a week, they talked of little else. The rest is rehearsal:
war might break out, or stop—next year, this time, it happens again.

Moving In

You scoured the fridge and rubbed at the blackened
dado rail. I washed out the cupboards
and laid down Contact, then took the old delft and scrubbed
through layers of years-old dirt and grease:
to an unchipped mug that's emblazoned
with "LA Olympics" and white athletes breasting the line;
to a side plate with green hem and lettering that spells:
"The Republican Party—Óglaigh na hÉireann;"
to the remains of a life, what smells
of a heavy smoker, a fire of some kind,
freebies, dereliction, febrile loneliness,
something that has waited years for another witness,
that re-approaches presence now we've cleared away room
for our new table and chairs, for ghosts to roam.

A Night In

I cook, you arrive, we eat, then do the ware,
I turn the washing machine to dryer mode
and we watch TV as the room heats up. What else?
You use the phone, we talk about what's on
or going on, our life, these walls—our world, and then
we reach for the remote. In the bedroom
you've pulled the curtains clear on either side
and hung your denim dress and my red shirt
on the curtain rail—with the window
and the cool, flickering city behind them
it looks as if they're waiting for us to nod off
before they desert our bodies
like a dream and float into the night.

The Find

The borrowed double ladder shifted
and I laid my hand on a bulb that I switched
at its base to light up the attic,
a dusty cave with uneven piles of bric-à-brac
and in the farthest corner stacked wooden grids,
the parts of a dismantled cot,
the kind we had put off buying for luck:
I carried down the lot, and out the back
you scrubbed clean the old wood,
inserted new screws and mild steel rods
what ran through the rail so that it all reared
up again on its own legs, the baby's bed
we'll lift into the spare room, but now, look,
reach into it, the space it makes.

The Calm

Into it they rush, frantic from the seasonal muzak,
the slashed prices and deceiving sizes,
draped with plastic bags and doing the new shoe shuffle
past the top-hatted doorman at the Imperial
who commands the footpath and waves at his friend in the truck

as a bride leaves and the wind picks up briefly
to rake crisp bags and drink cans
through car parks, past shopfronts and the cashpoint
we queue at behind men who ask women "Are you mad?"
before lighting out of it for sports bars and the big match.

It defines an eddy of dust at City Hall, invisibly,
and also the "Body Mind Spirit" signpost
where a cluster of young women and a solitary man
stand around smoking and examine the sky
for news of the next hour's inclination.

In Shalom Park a man shouts at a dog that won't stop barking,
a boy bangs a flat ball off the gable of the end house
and birds look down their beaks of wood at us,
at the city banked above the valley, sure of itself,
as if eternally there to reflect calmly

on the drifts of leaves and branches
where the river relaxes into the sea,
the terraced yards where our neighbors unpeg the washing
and talk about gardens and a good drenching
and—big drops pock the tar—the storm that's slowly approaching.

The Black Flower

He told me there was something I must see
and led me from the street and out the road
till we entered by a wooden stile a field
and, near this field's other side that banked steeply
to water, he vanished—as I was about to say,
"But this is just a hole in the ground."

Today's Imperative

after Horace, Ode 1.7

Others have herblife, bogland, the bird sanctuary.
Or man-made canals and urban decay.

And they have international flights of fancy too:
but wherever they go

it all looks and sounds the same to me,
mountains, some work, a nice sunrise that none of the
                              other tourists sees

or an epiphany that signals a deeper
engagement with the local patois/native literature.

Then there are the argonauts
who labor in the interstices of a language, or two at most;

and that crowd whose ambition is to introduce gender
to the reader who hasn't got one on him:

long warm-ups, agreed movements from *a* to *b*, and put up the shutters
with a lyrical turn or various little-known fabrics and figures,

such as you often find in those who use family detail as glitter
to stud the rough black rock of their fictions.

And I like all this, but
it doesn't live in me, it doesn't wake me up in my skin at night.

I'd rather sing to you about what's imperative,
so, listen. Take your mind off the stresses and anxiety of life

and whether you're in a southern town
like Cork or Montpellier, or even Washington or Rome—

go pour yourself a glass of wine.
Now. Imagine the kind of man who trusts himself to fortune

and says: "Let us go wherever it takes us.
We've heard that a better life awaits us *and* we've seen worse.

Today, banish worry, exile it, the night's young now
and soon we'll be back to the grind, in fact, maybe tomorrow…"

Action

It is 3 a.m., on a wet night, and I'm
in the middle of a field,
listening to *The Open Mind*, a repeat, on a Walkman
when Corman with his wand and loudspeaker cone
directs me, "Hey you," and then the long arm,
to walk across the field,
and to wade into the river
with the boom close to the water.
This is experience and I need experience.

The Gods

for Fionnuala Dillane

First out, the organist turns his back
to the slowly filling hall, places a compact
on the organ lid and carefully checks
the view, like the driver of a massive artic.

Everyone watches for time to be called.

The conductor's hands, a typewriter's ink wands,
touch choir and players—the sound of ink
rings through the concert hall, the mind's
survived by strings, brass, voices, woodwind.

An hour—in the gods we can see the musicians
turn to the last, blank page, the final rest,
and know in advance the silence before applause.

The audience, a blur of red and blue till now, lift
out of their seats, all faces and a flurry of hands.

Effects

On my one visit to your bijou apartment—
glass, wood, neutral tones—you went on
and on about important places you'd lived in,
then hushed the room to listen
to a bitter night in wartime Berlin

when snow unmapped streets
outside a hall bright with human heat
where an orchestra played Mozart
and a choir sight-read sheets
that gave the text a fresh start,

"Hic in terra" for "in Jerusalem,"
"Deus in coelis" for "Deus in Sion."
Through the static the boys' voices sound divine
and the crowd listen as if *Requiem*
was made with their night in mind.

You refilled our glasses and whispered
in my ear. As the announcer declared
"That was…" you flicked on your CD,
"Epic Effects," first up a yowling Arctic wind
rushed up my spine, then cold

wincing rain, a thunderstorm that
set me a-bristle like a cat
and your *pièce de résistance*, an at-
om bomb that I hear yet,
all jangle and unnatural collapse

with stringed seconds of nothing,
then the whole bone china teacup asunder,
a swinging door creaking open.
What night could go further?
I said my piece, not that you'd hear anything,

and walked home, in the rain and wind,
wondering at what exact point
the day becomes night
in a landscape like that, like this, light
disappearing from what's still left behind.

NEXT DOOR (2007)

A Pyramid Scheme

An old Cortina's come to rest
at the end of the road. The weeks pelt
its glass and steel, invisibly
emptying it and making free

with some random person
who strips the interior and then,
accompanied, helps himself
to tires, battery, driveshaft, exhaust.

The bodywork flakes and scabs.
Going nowhere, looking naked, mad,
mirrorless and windowless,
it gathers accessories

like one of those disused roadside crannies:
plastic bags, a seatful of empties
and, adjacent, a holed mattress, a pallet,
a small fridge—the whole lot useless, inside out,

till the rusting shell starts half-stories,
the kind that make it first notorious—
for the children who will have to learn
what goes on at night, or could go on,

then a shelter for their elders,
a try-out zone, its vacant doorless
frame a guarded hiding place, its fag-end
still paying a dividend.

Moving In

Her garden, once a selling point, is a state already.
Its furthest, dampest end is conifers, debris
and constant dark. And it's a zoo of noise,
sucking road and sky into the old semi's acoustic shadow.
There used to be one long bed of cultivated earth,
planted with care and effort,
where she—the last owner-occupier—
matched each half-season to a different color

so that one unknown variety ceded ground
to another unheralded
profusion of whites or reds or blues,
much as her post continues
to arrive, credit card and book club promotions
giving way to seasonal round robins
bearing good news, best wishes and written postscripts
from the colonies' retiring outposts.

Now I hardly step or look outdoors,
riveted by the school and fiscal years'
eternal returns, but unable to ignore
how one good neighbor or another
declares with careless, proprietary accent,
"She loved that garden," as I half-plan
uprooting even the roses to put in
here a slide, and there a swing.

Diversion

I noticed it day one and then forgot
the redbrick viaduct

till the Council boys
in the luminous hardhats and vests

raised scaffolding that cast shadows
straight and precise

as a map of the colonies
across the footpath and the green margin

where they've stacked the new sleepers
and earthed the transformer.

The Street

Lee's car has sat on blocks at least six weeks.
He rolls off the tarp and we stand around his yard.
His friend Amit, he reckons it's the sparks.
Then Mr. Kumar shuffles by, leaning on his stick,
with a can of petrol. He feeds it into his Bluebird,
straightens up and says, "Nice day. Will get hotter."
The rubbish is beginning to stink. The Council's on strike.
Kids suddenly mill around, chasing after
one another, and then they're gone again.
We mind our own business, no one says anything.
Mr. Kumar enters his front garden,
gone a bit to seed, and the lawn needs mowing.
We pretend we are all looking at Lee's defunct car,
me, Lee, Amit, even David whose window clicks
open across the street. It's melting; is it the sun
that's stopped moving, or us? Mr. Kumar darkens the front door,
faces up to its fish-eye lens, fingers his useless key
and presses the bell. The street goes quiet and sounds empty.
It seems to wait a minute, as if something
is about to repeat itself, even though there's no sign yet
of that door snapping open, of Mrs. Kumar
with a stick or a rolled-up paper to fold and switch the air
 around her husband's bowed and balding head, no sign
of his noise that goes nowhere but will fetch the large white van
and a policewoman, no sign either of how we'll start again
to speak to Mr. Kumar about the weather, or the state of the road
and the chances of driving it in his Bluebird or Lee's Colt.

Day Job

The routine
is so entrenched and second nature
that a deviation like last night's party
which ended with your missing the night bus
and walking miles home in the snow
throws you right off

and you're still
so dustily numb and dazed from its after-effects
you can hardly tell if the day's grind has happened
or you are still walking home in the snow
wondering how on earth
you'll get through tomorrow.

The Middle Kingdom: A Directory

For Receptions, Occasions and Venues, see the University, the Contact, Urmston Masonic Hall. "Bowl a maiden over at the Lancashire County Cricket Club." See Wedding Services. See Food. See Photos and Videos. See Clothes and Appearance. See Transport. See Religious Organizations.

For Religious Organizations, see also Churches, Church Halls and Places of Worship. See Church Furnishings and Supplies.

For Church Furnishings, see Reclaimers and Architectural Antiques. See also Builders' Merchants, Demolition, Roofing Materials, Salvage and Reclamation, Masons.

For Masons, see Monumental Masons, Memorial Stone Masons, Drystone Wallers and Sculptors.

For Sculptors, see Pop Empires and Bright Morning Star (or widen search).

For Bright Morning Star, see also under Calligraphy.

For Calligraphy, see Books, Rare and Secondhand, Factory Shops and Villages (See also Further Education; see Universities). See also Shopping Centers. See Decorations.

For Decorations, see Costumes, see Fancy Dress, Theatrical Supplies, Uniforms and Staff Wear.

For Uniforms and Staff Wear, see also Marking and Other Identity Services, see Barcodes, see Rubber Stamps, see Security Services and Equipment.

For Security Services and Equipment, see also Intercom Systems. See Closed Circuit TV and VTR. See Hi-fi. See Gifts.

For Gifts, see Flowers, see Garden Centers (See Nurseries, see Decorations), see also China and Glass (Crystal). See Wedding Services. See also Places of Worship, Church Furnishings, Masons, Sculptors, Decorations, Flowers. See The Moon Under Water for England's Finest Venues and Occasions. See The Chorlton Conservative Club, see The Black Lion (No Reception).

Interview

I read an interview
       where she talked about
how the most important,
       the lodestar events
of her life to date
       had not been the sort
which an image
       or a storyline
might, on average,
       be said to define
but instead rested
       at the fringe
of what might have been
       in the…
And she broke off
       or I was called from the queue,
singled out, like anyone,
       for a treatment
to which I alone
       would be subjected.

Interference

I step into it as it surrounds me,
a patch of earth so hemmed in by trees
the branches meet over my head.
Another person, like a curtain in a sick ward,
draws the little light into her interfering voice.
What she says is nothing new:
"It will all come out in the wash."
A stout short woman, of high color,
she must drink alone at night
with that same narrow look of desire.

Will she still be there—a secret keeper—afterwards?
She'd said, "I'm keeping my eye on you."
I thought I saw her at an uncle's funeral,
and that day we moved house. I like to hear
little or nothing about her.
All this time, too, I feel
the damp heat rising out of the earth,
the wind shaking down the trees.

Tinnitus

My father's tinnitus is like the hiss off a water cooler,
only louder. And it doesn't just stop like, say, a hand dryer—the worst is
it comes and goes. Or you shine a light on it
and it looks permanent as the sea,

a tideless sea that won't go away. The masker
he's been prescribed is a tiny machine, an arc of white noise
that blacks out a lot
but can't absorb the interference totally

any more than you or I—taking the air,
stirring milk into coffee, daydreaming through the six o'clock news,
trying to sleep on a wet night—
can simply switch off what's always there, a particular memory

nagging away, the erosive splash off a little river
wearing away the road, say, on the Connor Pass,
a day out, through which he'd accelerate
in the flash, orange Capri.

By Accident

The night our boy fell I was running late.
I made the unanswered call
under the city's bright,
then cloudy, skull
and, as the needle knows the north,

trembled at the shock ahead,
a house blacked-out and silent,
a night that, commuted,
ran to earth in accident,
a shorted circuit, you and he locked

into the diagnostic dark
in Park Royal intensive care
where consequences arc
beyond "contusion," "fracture,"
the ward's humming network

to a different city, a year later,
the kind of night, calm, almost tranquil,
when he calls and haggles with his sister
even as we find more and more unreal
our imaginings, which were terrible.

The Yard

The yard can no more be split in two
than the house it backs onto
or is backed onto by.
In one corner a small, red-cheeked boy
looks through the fence's eye-sized hole
as if his yard is no more the whole
of the wide world
than the ball his red-haired sister has whirled
over the washing line
which acts today as a dividing line
across the muddy, green, uneven ground
and gives him grounds
to turn his back
even as his sister calls him back
to where, as things get out of hand,
the ball will land
on still-disputed land.

The Low Road

I turned back
and took the ferny, lower fork,
a return that veered towards a river sound
which itself seemed wound at a steeper arc
down to some deeper, blacker sound.

A deer backed clear,
its scut like a child's upturned nose,
and sprang away from the grass road
into a flurry of higher grass
up the pass

to the town's environs;
I should have followed, higher in the valley,
closer to the sky,
far from the anxiety
of that drifting moraine

of leaves and dusty pine cones
which felt as if it would give way,
the year's mossy detritus
a locally made
subsidized softness,

the tall and fallen trees
fording what might have been the river
not even a mile
from a knot of houses,
almost a village… But that was later:

first the sky would disappear,
the ground flatten to a cliff, bare and awkward
as a shadow on a small black river,
the same river that, as long as I walked,
I would not see but only hear.

The Deep North

The weather is coming down around them and filling up the fields
but they are Sunday drivers, stuck in a dead end, with their heads
buried all the while in table-sized road maps that approximate
to where they live, in what we'll call the Hall of the Present Life,
its walls loud and impermeable as radio and its roof screwed shut
so they rarely notice the emissaries of the Hall of the Western Paradise
who dwell among them at crossroads, in courtyards and country lanes,
who take many guises, whose form is fluid and inconstant,
who will receive the souls of the dying believers,
who on their vests wear the names of those who paid for their creation,
who carry in one hand a rope for binding, and in the other a knife.

The Graveyard

The trees
in their ivy ballgowns
state the obvious

but the irregular stones
upright or at an angle
are unimprovable:

they gesture and whisper
 about seeing no future
in peace or rest.

The formal lawn
is so even
it's almost not there.

Painted a glossy black,
the ornate gate
creaks and shines.

Clouds

Where I sit—in the uncovered stand,
beside me my copy of Han-Shan—
might as well be the east face of Cold Mountain:
the rain rolls in, in waves. But let's stop
looking at the clouds. The ball's about to hop,
one man moves his feet fierce and quick:
the crowd, too late and almost to itself, shouts "Pull."

Beyond the posts, the planes, their vapor trails
lost in the clouds. Myself, I puck the odd ball
in back garden and public park,
once in a retired stadium, the grass knee-high,
vague and excessive as a cloudy sky.
A baby's crying ceases. It's a good connection.
Away it sails.

The Quiet Life

Is it this you wanted, the still center
of the quiet life, its ticking clock,
the white goods' hum and on/off click,
next-door's pipes and creaking stair?
It could be, let's face it, anywhere,
the usual birds sleep in its shadow
and from every side, in stereo,
a surf of noise going who knows where,
traffic clutching, flown, a landing plane,
the trains' two-beat come and go…
And outside the mirrored window,
closer to home, in the tended garden
and the undergrowth, what rustles
there, or in its wake, might be
grass stirring or, on *their* way,
even your discarded half-read papers.

You Interrupt

Purr and whistle, a change of gears,
the milk float, next-door's shift and the chorus
of robin, tit and blackbird: all have read
our waking up. "Nearly 5," you said,
"and it's already bright." The children stirred,
but didn't wake: things could be worse.
Real coffee for an early start. The word
for this is long-lost, beyond use: it'll be years,
and what harm, before it gets a chance.
You interrupt, "It's not like this:
it's the same as before;" birdsong, the steaming kettle…
Upstairs first one, then the other begins to call.
Is this enough? Will that be alright?
You'll go in a while; the traffic's still light.

**** **** **** 5443

I'm held in the second bar
of the Revenue's *Casio* solo,
the hot receiver at my ear,
drumming the stairs with my free hand,
on my lap a sheaf of credit card statements,
like a book of lyrics,
each with a number and date, some named:
The Lime Tree, The Bookshop, Dove Cottage.
Dove Cottage: it's as if I'm miles away,
not many moons ago, escaping a traffic jam,
walking up that dusty, cobbled sidestreet,
a dwarf orchard at one corner,
music too, from an open doorway,
money in my pocket, time on my hands.

A Minute

The Fog Lane short cut is barred by a tree chipper,
an army of legless conifers, and a trail of tinsel
and broken ornaments. The sky turns copper
and I start to remember how the rain would pour
at New Year's meetings in Limerick and Tramore.
But before the downpour, before I throw in the towel,
before I fumble, in two minds, for the mobile
and directions, I've a minute to consider
the roads Sunday-quiet, the bagels as yet unbought,
and how this day's carry-on seems now customary
as the new eruvs of Temple Fortune where, on Shabbat,
train lines and back-alleys host activity
undreamt of by the old Law on whose holy day
the baby should cry and cry, the meal burn dry,
speech disappear and even news of this stay put.

Town

We leave tomorrow and the night finds me—where else—
down by the river, its current quiet and regular as a pulse,
silvery dark where the banked trees grow around
the outflow pipes. A bird takes off and goes to ground
in a commuter's site whose unpainted cement
is either half-finished or half-dismantled.
Farther off I see, bright as an oil rig, the Co-op shine
and foam, humming its bottom line.

Empty river, indifferent night: no joke.
We'll leave, grow older, return, say, "Then what?"
On it all the glowing river twists the ground shut.
The town's lit up, but no one comes back to reminisce,
intent as some evangelist smashing fossils,
making a religion out of feeling homesick…

Hedge

1. The Onion Harvest

You face me from one end
of the long waist-high hedge
like a train driver looking down
the barrel of his engine

but bare-chested, on holiday,
captaining this green train
that you've draped
with strings of onions

each green-brown, testicular bulb
like a light socketed from the earth
shining its spot or ball light
out of the glistening hedge

into the fir screen's grey-blue shadow
and your own grey, brown torso.

2. Road Safety

I check the convex mirror in the hedge across the way
and see, beyond plantations of fir and rowan,
the roadside monument to the killings
of 1918 and 1921
and, up the road, away from this house on its bed
of unraveled blue pencil and its hill of water,
the empty crossroads for Knocknagoshel and Duagh,
and from the hedge that frames this convex mirror,
wild with blackberries, gooseberries,
dribbling mice, a hen pheasant will soon wander
 the grassy margin, among the thistles
and the ragwort and the nettles,
and will halt there a while, quiet out,
seeing time pass, looking in every direction.

The Hundred Towns

"There is no capital of the world."
—*Czesław Miłosz, "Bypassing Rue Descartes"*

We negotiate
      ring road, tunnel and ferry
            but by noon GMT

are nowhere, i.e., an endless suburb
      stacked and balanced
            like washing-up.

The day out seems set to fray
      into a relief map of noise,
            the kids crying *where*

until you call a halt
      and we abandon the car
            and follow a sign pointing east:

we reach the beaten path, tar and mud,
      and trundle buggies up blind, rising corners,
            piggyback past tourists consulting an *A–Z*

and a man with children who smiles
      at the sight of us:
            "another day in paradise…"

In a mile, an hour, we lay out the picnic,
      a tartan rug on the side of a hill,
            greenly adrift in the public park:

a barbecue smokes the wind,
      a lean-to of a caff
            hosts wake-up karaoke, blues and big band

(someone murders "It's oh so quiet"),
      quad bikes buzz and weave
            earning a crowd with their figures of eight

and across the river Canary Wharf glitters,
      a sky-high shower curtain
            in the rainless weather.

Quick clouds flit in the sky's corners.
      Flat out in the heat like a film,
            the city's empty, the future of a hundred towns.

The kids run off; we share a cold and fizzy beer,
      but I close my eyes as you say, "We could not,
            would not be anywhere but here,"

and I sleep off this well-planned afternoon
      a mile above, and hours beyond
            the trail's blazing, sawdust line…

OF ALL PLACES (2011)

Old Style

Not just the lay-by, or the motorway
       or its central reservation.
Not just the ring road, or the cul-de-sac
       with its pretty forsythia border.
Not just the house, or its extension,
       and its hundred windows shining away.
Instead the known world and the unseen,
       to which you'll come back:

that is, the point of departure, the destination,
       and all points in between.
A free drift to nowhere in particular.
       All that way, and back again.

The Coming Times

The towns are not so dark that no one enters;
in nearby docks the nights
advance on empty lots.
Fanatics gather in community centers.

A dry spell engenders nostalgia for rain.
The news will consider
the negligent doctor
and who is immune to the variant strain.

In cooler queues low-slung jeans
date the waspie;
the bright bars are smoke-free
as the ocean's photic zones.

The downturn floats the clearance sale:
staff migrate
and the market
anticipates no return; churches fill,

the ice cap melts, the deserts spread:
north and south
a dolphin's found in every port;
new forms of algae feather the tide.

The boats will travel day and night
and some make land.
For the time being, out of mind
is out of sight:

from the dawning dark
no one shouts, no walk-outs.
Someone organizes scouts,
someone patrols the park.

Bringing the Baby to Rossaveal

If the real world is not altogether rejected
                                        —W. B. Yeats

The field is a limestone heat sink. A goat
and a pony stretch where stone walls meet.
The sea wind is head-high or, at the five-barred gate,
a passage we brave to the open pub. A wet May
and a dry June. The traffic. The roads. Not a cock of hay.
Goodbye to the first times, goodbye Galway.

Under adjoining, improvised trestles, folded into
her awkward car seat, the baby sleeps through
Germans to whom we speak French poorly,
the house red, a mug or two of coffee
and the sun making light of the menu.
Goodbye to the first times, goodbye Galway.

Pushing the squeaking buggy to the B&B
I overlook her quick inquiring glances at the moon
as I try to recall, going through Security
with my shoes undone, what is stowed away
among recycled shopping bags in the undercarriage—
Goodbye to the first times, goodbye Galway—

a bottle, a banana, in this, the softest year and day
of living, anyway, our Lord, in the institution of marriage,
the sun at night, Galway under the volcano of dawn
we fly into, one time, with everything else at bay,
the baby squeaking, like the small wheel, the sun gone down.
Goodbye to the first times, goodbye Galway.

Badgers

During training, on the Cows Lawn, one of the smokers,
a boy from Ballylongford, coughed up blood, black clots of it.
We stood on the sidelines till he was taken away.
This was the time O'Hare, the Border Fox, was on the loose.
That day, arriving home from school, who didn't promise
he'd never ever take a pull again? Not in the school bog,
not in the back way, not in the fag-breaks at the petrol station.
But another rumor released us. It was the farm and badgers:

brock, feral, slow-clawed terror of the ditch and yard,
wind-pissing shit-spreader, emptier of field and house.
Its fellow travelers, then as now like garrulous crows,
swore the opposite, the blood-dregs nothing
to their stone-silent survivor, always in the right,
and us and the herd safer. Or so they put it about even as,
barely visible behind the numbers, old tales resurged
about loosened fence posts and sloping, scraped-up footpaths.

O'Hare could not be found by the guards: that smokeless week
I stood in the porch (under a new, secure intercom)
rubbing a leaf between my thumb and index finger,
noticing a little movement in a Volkswagen
parked, as it had been all along, past the last gate,
as if this were a garage forecourt and not
a dead end, a river facing it, its animal sentries
unvisited as those on many another road.

Continuity

The wind sails leaves around the house like late notices
of the garden's deterioration. Turn a blind eye.
RTÉ longwave announces gigs in familiar venues.
I like the presenter's comfortable thoughts of tonight
and the day after, until, that is, he introduces
"The Holy Land" by the Bothy Band and then
advertises a poetry broadsheet and a silver plaque,
before attacking, quote, the crimson tides
and purple mountains, end quote, someone (who?)
might waste his money on instead in Woolworths.
There's a snatch of a shipping forecast
and I'm unloading the dishwasher when I hear a new voice,
which strands me by announcing, "This is *The Archive Hour*,
and that was *The Long Note* thirty years ago today,"
out of earshot as I am of the autumn sun and rain
which the radio forecasts, too, on this hour that's gone
south with its silver plaque, its piano and *bodhrán*,
where, in Woolworths, a crimson tide progresses
beneath a purple mountain and someone hums a reel.
He knows the start of it but puts a question mark
against the title: it's "The Holy Ground" but he doesn't join the dots.
He has places to go. There will be time again for names and dates,
for taking it all down, for credits, for footnotes.

The Listowel Arms

The silver, Georgian teapot he presented to her—
is it still in Chequers, or did she take it home to Finchley?
He meant civil conversation, talks,
but was not unhappy, says a biographer,
when the hacks construed it as the boss
putting the grocer's daughter in her woman's place,
the grocers' sons suiting the occasion to the usual offense.

I saw him twice. At a hotel opening,
with a woman who might have been his daughter,
and a school half-day when I'd skipped training
and was cycling home. I came on
an unexpected crowd, where I saw not a one
of my friends and classmates, investors in the future
of systems analysis and the virtual share

but, like a captain on the night of a match day,
this small, bustling, jostled colonel
of William and Market Streets, surrounded on Mart Day
by hundreds of men, a river of tweed.
I veered up the back way, though, and turned
for the Square where, after his scandal, the town saw Parnell
at a window in the *Arms* make his final biblical call,

"Thus far shalt thou go," before taking tea in that same bar
where the merchants still rendezvous for elevenses,
between the town's churches and the unrestored castle
which I skidded by, chancing a breather
near the racecourse bridge's damp concrete angle
which rubbed BRITS OUT and the Malvinas
up against *who* loved *who* and sex cartoons,

the river pouring under, a nightfall of rain on its back,
absorbing the west Limerick and Co-op surplus,
wheeling it all past the town's built-up backyards,
the Island's empty racetrack
and this tire-spinners' gravel car park,
the town's learners practicing turns and how to reverse,
the heat and 2FM turned up to the max.

Aerialist

i.m. Vitaly Kharapavitski

I'd talked us all back to Ireland, a week in Killorglin and a plan
to take shovel, bucket, armbands and an inflatable fin,
a picnic basket and a tartan rug to a different beach
each mid-morning. It was quiet and all worked out, so much
we might have dreamed it and never gone—except
that one day we parked on Inch Strand and plowed it up
as the tide around us did what it does.

Cooped up inside at night was a different prospect
in a rental no one could pretend was Bali or Venice.
For entertainment, ice-cream vans and posters for a circus,
not exactly an infrastructure. The "Royal Russian Circus:"
20 euro a head. I cursed the Celtic Tiger and paid, cash at the till,
wishing briefly I'd stayed, done an MBA and, some violence
to the language, lived it deal by deal.

Every artist looks after his own props. The balloon
"exploded into flames," the cage fell, then the heavy steel ball.
Becoming witnesses, one or two hundred people
thought it was part of the act, fire as magic, whoosh and clatter,
nothing irregular in the mid-air routine.
The reports say he was Belorussian, 26, a clown or
"an aerialist in a clown costume." And that he threw his wife clear.

We'd seen, in Rosbeigh, pre-show and a week earlier,
hanging around, nerveless and going nowhere an elephant,
a giraffe and, between them, a zebra. Canvas and steel
were shaped into a marquee. And from behind Coomasaharn
glider after glider hung in the sky, coasting away clear to the north.
A new bungalow advertised art, another a scuba school
and night-kayaking in the phosphorescent ocean

by which that night, stars and stripes on each enormous brow,
the elephants balanced on buckets like shuttlecocks,
while the giraffe nodded, stately and gawky, and a shabby lion
made his unheard-of roar, still a memory on each nearby farm.
A crowd of method actors, the circus animals, though
instead of a tiger the MC, for the sake of form,
squirted water at us from a flower between acts.

The "Sadovs" had performed for one year and had one stunt:
in it he couldn't find her, she fooled and hid,
the story so simple we gripped the wooden ringside,
grinding our heels into the matted grass and, would it ever end,
opened our mouths like parents as he kept
falling over and out of the hot-air balloon. Over
and over he went, *poor man*, who would throw his wife clear.

Weeks later, and back across the water, I saw online
the Dublin owner of the Royal Russians, or its spokesman,
speak of close-knit community, the harness, the hoist,
and the families of the deceased and bereaved flying over.
It seemed for a while, here, as if things might be as they were,
autumn closing in, a net that at the last moment would come apart
taking only the leaves from the trees and the name of the year.

A Mountain Road

The visitor explained how to make "A Mountain Road:"
as in the original, a line of sea, the road and fields,
which some of us personalized. His had a black hill,

which those without black paint painted a very dark green.
You couldn't tell the difference when he tacked
all twenty-eight versions of "A Mountain Road"

high around the drafty classroom which now recedes
stone by stone into its own mountain road,
the hill beside it black and visible, beyond its empty fields

and new forestry, the lighthouse on Loop Head
whose cone of light sweeps across the soft grey shore
and seems, minute after minute, to find and inspect it.

My Adolescence in New Zealand

for Bill Manhire

I didn't want to go to bed and then
I didn't want to get up. The men,
my uncles and father, planned to watch
the international, a grudge match,
on the new remote-controlled TV.
I was beginning to get ideas about coffee.
I sniffled and coughed, my nose in a book.
The *Rainbow Warrior* turned into Helen Clark.
Those days we worried about serious things.
I was never into *The Lord of the Rings*.
I preferred biographies of polar explorers:
a long journey and evidence of errors
disappearing like a snowflake in Antarctica,
a dropped knife tuning up for the orchestra.

Jane Eyre in Derry

Seven hours with Charlotte Brontë
on the Galway-Sligo bus to Derry
and on arrival, reader, it would be hard not
to have a problem with the shut, shuttered pubs,
the early closing of unknown bookshops,
the picketed cinema not screening *Prêt-à-Porter*,
the black cab's same old uncongenial story...
But I'm happily lost in writing a list
at the loose end of your shift
when here you are, you and the bright air
of your short, boyish haircut
which you wear, in Altnagelvin,
like an amulet
to stop roughly half the staff knowing
what they believe in.

Week 2

Let the books outstay their return date.
Let it be said that we are sleeping late.
Let the garden continue to grow more like a dump.
Let the room go cold round this mid-season slump.
Let scientists be someone else's concern
as their particles accelerate slowly at CERN.
Let today's headlines give no one the hump.
Let the friendlies occur to some other chump.
Let the weather be forecast, the Dow deflate.
Let the sun go down and the moon circulate.
Let milk sour in the fridge, and the cream turn.
Let nothing happen, again, except you return.

Batman

At the same secure gate, after the interview,
I met you with your new retinue

who, over drinks in *The Rising Sun*,
explained things, then needled us about Irish abortion,

as private a matter as that lab
that no one would mention. But you took the job

and we phoned around,
praised medical science's miracle fund,

their pledge to back whatever your research examined.
The art deco reading area was like a deep end

in the library's converted pool.
There were poems and new paintings on every wall.

One unglamorous year later
the site, on the green belt, was under the hammer:

Christopher Nolan shut the place down
and spent two weekends shooting *Batman*,

his *Gotham* vans a nice change from the unmarked cars
used to film, each Wednesday, the protesters,

who filmed them, of course, in return.
That was the Wednesday cat-and-mouse routine,

the necessary taxi, drummed on,
given dog's abuse by the committed and the vegan

till you forgot, once, and walked out the main gate,
"the last time," you said at home, shaken and in no state.

A Likeness

        The wind makes itself known
in the laurel, a soft buffeting of the washing on the line;
the ivy on the fence is veined with lime
and starts its terraced nodding at a lower breeze
which brings with it the cabbage white and the admiral.

Now the two winds come at once, the buffeting
and the ivy turned downside up, sea-green,
the fence a little visible and, overhanging it all,
the brambles, blackberries on their tongues pale green and pink
and black with tiny straw hooks. Picked ripe, they grow back.

Influence

Let's stick, you say, to describing what *is*,
weather ridged like a dune, blown into angles
like whipped, whitened cream, then brown-on-grey
like frozen muddy fields animals trample.
The deck and the deck furniture a window display,
cake slices and muffins with overwhelming icing,
the sort kids like the look of but won't eat.
We chance town, an obstacle course,
for the banquet in *Ocean Harbor*,
our only company tanks of eels, crabs and lobsters.
Trees creak in the wind, lined and ermine,
as we raise a beer to the idea of influence,
the Year of the Tiger and learning acquiescence
to the weather, an icicle that grows and tapers,
a stiletto blur of blue and grey.

                    But its solid forms, the day after,
tire like memory, depleted and depleting,
not the same thing at all now and in the way,
its scuffled pages another recognizable allusion
to what might be the case another day,
meltwater pooling in tire tracks and footprints.

Marriage, the Realist Tradition

There are introductions. A letter arrives. Already
we sympathize with the solitary reader, the interrupted study
in a house no one visits. Who would want to?
We are gripped by an idea, a pilgrimage turns into
a road trip. In the awful weather monsters shrink and, indoors,
assume human forms. We might grow into these foyers and porches.
Where were we? The twin no one ever knew returns.
A mysterious stranger's glance means a head turns.
It is a gaze we follow; now, an inheritance or marriage
is in the balance. New laws or wars throw a shadow, like knowledge,
on what used to happen, but won't ever happen again. Is this
the improbable lift-off into another world, like and unlike life?
Illness sudden as eclipse, or that famous intervention—
love—makes impossible a life of their own invention.
A misunderstanding, a wrong name taken to heart?
No place here for the bad student considering art
but the novelists, the last to specialize in everything, produce
with the frenzy of an enormous unselfconscious youth
a city like a farm, and characters with something to say or
something to hide and, later, a denouement, on the moor
or in the car park, foreshadowed with subtle hints, maybe this
the improbable lift-off into another world, like and unlike life?
Someone's paying attention to the weather, its big picture;
there is an etymological diversion, an old man (someone's father?)
who retells or invents (will they, won't they?) the monstrous past.
A letter arrives (stop describing the clock—her mother's)—open it!
We sit around a table, old and flat and round,
waiting for the girls and the boys to arrive, then head in hand,
no longer talking, we're discovered by the same old story. The plot
creaks into place around us, a picture frame gilded and ornate,
too neat and a little too close to whatever we call home,
which is where (we saw it coming) she takes his name,
stitching everyone into the same black and white pattern
and, somewhere off the page, an ending we believe in.

Sunrise

There are nights I snag on a single morning—
lodged where it can't be got rid of—
a boy, the local poet's son, arrived so late
I threatened a visit to the Head
and got, in return, a sleepy reply:
"My father, sir, took me to Knockanure
to wait for the dawn—to see the sun."

He drew me a picture later, a line
like a brim or a lid or a shade.
Mortal thoughts our mutual friends:
no sign of the sun, the frost a web of mist.
More than ever I like to see
what's in front of me and nothing else.

By the Sea, in England

for Conor O'Callaghan

It's not like the lip or verge of anything.
There are no surfers here who paddle and balance
to where a reef splits the currents
into a wave's right-angle.
Instead beachcombers stockpile
driftwood, or sieve for fossils and a king's shilling;

and heavy machinery, for the links or the farmer,
ships inland
industrial loads of seaweed and sand;
seagulls gabble and scramble up,
into the gale, at the sight of a ship
from Santander;

residents walk the pier, kick the wall
and, about-face, puff and windmill
one day into another.
No cold, spraying wind blows off this shore
like a monomaniacal point of view.
Its slow tides might as well be hung with snow.

It is windbreakers draped with striped towels,
the brisk noise in a sand dune's endless morning,
the flask and the sandwich, the breakers breaking
netless courts, names drawn with shovels,
the fortified castle and elaborate moat,
the dull shine off the tide's cloudy aftermath.

It's not like standing
at the lip or verge of something,
not here, where the sea peters out,
the rumor of a distant pool. But if it's not
that lisping, withdrawing crash on a bronze beach
it is, halfway to silence, this hush

which is, too, not just nothing
and carries across
the stony foreshore and the strand's fine grain
what could pass for a canal's stillness,
cyclists—familial, in single file—cresting
the sea-defense's low and wavy bank. Their inland tune.

Transfers

On the sale of works of art from the Bank of Ireland collection, 24 November 2010

Their backs to the crowded quay, a couple sails away from the regatta:
in lakes nearby mountains reverse into the distances
and stones line up, in order, at the brink. Seen from another shore
the bay steadily darkens with the prospect of herring
and no sign of another boat to spread its net like a tablecloth
into the long night and the water ahead of it.

The red tractor idles in the yard when it should be in the field,
children wait in hand-knits and short trousers with the animals
or bring home fish in a galvanized bucket or turf on a white donkey,
bearing with them an autumn day. An old man raises his hand
and lapwings crowd around the house, its black rich soil and eggy sun,
a world known for the first time as they reel through Holyhead:
    why leave it all

for the creased benches of a vent-heated waiting room, a life
as at home with the cooling tower as the night ferry,
fixing devices unheard of in Borneo or Ballyconnell,
while the places they played in as children suddenly look skeletal
    and strange?
Years of birdsong are withdrawn into the folds of unusual drapery.
    Daffodils find
a vase on a sill, the city's trees are tangled capillaries, a memory

of a bank of thatch-colored cloud separated from thatched cottages
by a winding hill-bound lane they will drive on holiday,
one building dwarfing its neighbor, the entrances indistinct.
Whitewashed walls support turf, a ladder, a barrel, and their shadows:
    he sees her,

now they arrive, standing between windows, a blue dress against
    a blue pillar,
her white throat binding one thing into another, a soft dune of light.

By the sea, again, brighter but empty, the rocks develop a prowling
    quality
and, obeying another law of perspective, the couple stands before a
    rick of turf
as if it's the open bonnet of a touring vehicle, circa 1938:
hesitant bystanders at a fire sale, they stand apart
(she links her hands behind her back, he holds one lapel of his
    marsh-colored mac)
and stay together, the water and hills their own eternal
insubstantial history, grand ruined illusions of color and light.

On their wall the image of another wall, each tiny leaning stone
    almost free
of its companion. Under an expanding mountain the multiplying
    extensions,
disappearing yards and accreting kitchens foster unlikely foliage
as if each interior and side elevation were a facet of some murkily
    imagined freedom.
Domesticity burns itself into the rusty archive of coasts and edges,
trees disguise the horizon's bottom line, a scratched-out human figure,
    the field
a meadow of bluebells, a hare escaping a hound on the point of twisting
    it into the air.

A Name

The big window and beyond it again the flowering beanstalk and
    the climbing frame,
fountains of fern and a recovering buddleia. I'd like a name
for how these busy, so-called "hard-pressed servants of my will,"
    the years,
go by the by like forgotten days and half-remembered quarter hours.
Would naming it change anything? Evening, all shadow and charm,
    wanders by.
Among the wildflowers the beady strut and ratchet of a magpie.
Through the window come those go-betweens, the wasp and the fly.

Black Box

The stable I called a dungeon is the coal shed:
going there a "big production," my mother sighs,
starts in the living room. By the cold fireplace
I slip the tin caddy out of a "traditional" brass box,
its relief a bumpy picture I can feel and almost see,
a coach and horses from another century.

Soot gathers at the bottom like cornflakes
left over in the cereal box.
I pour it on the husks and ashes fallen through the grate,
then trail more soot—my name in my mother's mouth—
across the wet yard's muddy gravel
and start to scrape and clink the coal into the scuttle,

poking the coals into a black on black jigsaw puzzle,
practicing how to whistle and piece things together,
fine dust freezing back into some fantastic, original shape,
as I heft the lot, blacken the carpet—I still hear my mother—
and build a pyramid from paper twists and *Zip*,
the hoover going, damp hissing off the wet coal.

The Hallway Mirror

You walk by with an armful of school shirts.
The ironing. But where's he gone? He's
outside, a standing column in the air he breathes,
the snow general and the falling flakes his obedient recruits,
conscripting everything to the same white flag.
His sisters, wildcats, growl and laugh.
We unload the washing, kiss, relax into the indoor arts
till the open door admits him in a crinkled fog,
wearing the usual get-up, marrying a word to life.

A Midgie

I pick a midgie out of my red wine.
The garden goes greener in the lilac time.
This will go down on the permanent record.
A night is nothing if not its own reward.
The foxgloves corked with bees.
The snail outlining a life of ease.
The black things wait. Or may never show.
That's innocent. I know, I know.

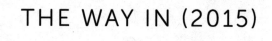

THE WAY IN (2015)

Very

It's a color
        it's walking in the dark
It's the road
It's a car we drove
        it's crying
alternately to
        it's trying
work and holidays
        it's a small dog you loved to juggle on your foot
In cities it's the beach
        it's a night
it's a glass of wine
        it's the morning and the radio
in a small glass
        saying something out loud, oblivious
There is more
        it's mid-afternoon, once in a while,
        it's very
        it's very you

Shed

for Peter Fallon

I bought the shed, for a song, off a neighbor
who'd stopped using it after he paved the garden.
He'd inherited it or got it somewhere he couldn't remember,
not that I gave a second thought to its origin.

It was heavier than it looked so he helped take the roof to pieces.
After an hour prying out each crooked tack
we levered off its grey-green sandpaper stiffness
and rested it, on the drive, like a book stranded on its back.

The neighbor, looking at his watch, said, "Let's push,"
and the four walls and floor did move—a little.
In front of the garage, sweating, feeling each
ounce of the previous night, we saw too late

it was too big to go through. We counted the nails but couldn't:
they were like stars, more the more we looked. "Heave it over,"
over the garage and down, he joked,
the garden path to its resting place under the magnolia.

No joke: we made a ramp of the ladder and inched
this half-ton pine crate up and out of the road.
The scraped-flat garage roof pitched
under our careful feet. Two euphoric beers later, after we'd lowered

it into place, we agreed on twenty quid. Every so often
he still calls in: today he's selling up and getting out.
He asks about the shed. I say it's fine, so half hidden
by April gusts of leaf and petal he can hardly see it,

as we look, out the window, at where it leans
against the fence, painted green, the unlocked door
opening on the lawnmower and half-full cans
of paint and petrol, pure potential, evaporating into the air.

But work makes work: paving the lot, he volunteers, makes more sense.
I'm offering him a cup of tea
when, before he can collect himself, he starts to resent
the twenty quid and leaving the shed behind: "It was," he says,
    "almost free."

Skin

A day nothing will darken:
in the shaded kitchen
a space clears as the leaf
of the table is lifted level.

And what is it in the silence
that appears? 1985, sand, towels
draped across the chairs,
her voice, arranging the place,

Ambre Solaire, his big shoulders
painfully hot and shedding skin
which rubs off as it is handled
or, under my fingernail,

peels away in thin,
papery patches. Sheer,
blurring wing-scraps
I look through.

Family Room

Here we are, the family room, my back-to-front
"Intro to Litho" coming up, as you might expect,
as "something" blue squeegeed into a frame
while you stage-manage the kids into an elegant line,
no longer the groom and bride, rosily afloat
over Russian peasants, nor yet the shark tanked and split,
nor those longing companions Poussin
stitches into the fringes of a citified garden,

though skipping the exhibition after, max, an hour
I see under the electrifying, blue-black velvet
umbrellas of an Impressionist underwriter,
a sudden, first look we occasionally visit.
Traffic can snarl all it wants around its blue.
In case you're ever wondering, I want to.

Echo

                    Pushing open the porch door
on what has nested behind it these many days,
it scrapes and catches as I bend down and away from
the milk bottles and bins to pick up the red cards
for missed deliveries, multiple copies of the "local" paper,
our MP's updates on cuts and parking,
takeaway offers and the glittering remnants of a gift
dropped on the tiled floor the night before I left

for Lisbon, sandcastles, a wave washing up on the shore,
buckets and spades, a puff of air in the high places,
ice-cream cones, a month coming closer and closer
to the end of its power, a celloish withdrawal
from the porch's altering air finding me at a loss,
patting jeans as the house key does not appear—
where is it I would be going? Or getting away from?
(A geography precise and confining as a childhood

that each inching away extends and deepens)—
no key emerging from under a mat or out of a pocket,
getting a laugh from knocking on my own door,
but not so much when, stepping out
to peer in the window, it sounds, on the other side,
as if someone's typing, the kettle's steaming and the drum
of the washing machine is rattling to, its willful belting on
followed by beeping, as if I've been, these many days, an echo,

right here really, of a life that has gone on, regardless,
beyond the floral spheres and bee violins August sucked
into a green square, its timbre and treble these many days
met by the industrial hum which worsens, cut with
that pejorative roaring that won't admit another,
the radio in the kitchen going on about what lies in store,
its right-or-wrong, "must be done," parental decibel
shouting down and amplifying what it would correct,

as I right myself in the drafty porch, locked out,
my silence a rail I would ride away from it.

                                        Let's.

Soft Landing

What will I be wearing?
A suit and tie, good shoes.

Rouge.
And an attempt at lipstick.

Will I have my glasses on?
And where will it rest,

this made-up body? Who with? My father
taking me to his mother's, "among what rushes"

on the far side of a new motorway.
We'd visit by walking across a field,

in a hurry till after, leaving Imphrick,
and not really seeing what she's missing.

Common ground. And for company?
I know. Morbid thought

forming around a star,
your hard fire:

I would be, now or at the hour,
in the dark alone first, counting that

another success:
Breathe the air and smile at this.

Reading this on the back of a letter
found in a shoebox in the shed
next to the wooden garden table
I've screwed back together for the summer.

The paper's creased carefully
at the folds, much considered once
but never sent from here
or copied, just put away

where it stirs in the shadow
of the unkillable linden,
lopsided and ragged
as if it's growing out a haircut:

a magpie—the national bird,
opportunist, a noise abroad—
perches on the table,
then on a skinny branch,

unsteady gauntlet it jumps off,
clambering among sweet spots,
soft landings, eager for light, forgetful
even in departures.

Longford Park

for Vona Groarke

The pavilion's deserted
and grass creeps
out of tarmac tennis courts.
Someone's been at the hedges.

An Afghan hound,
off the leash, on the loose,
lopes towards pigeons
and a blackbird. Dusk

and the gates close
on the last jogger. A minibus
turns on its lights
and heads for the city.

Over the south wall,
in the hidden garden,
the top of a bouncy castle
and, every so often, children.

From Here

The view from here is the border:
the lake, close-up, is vertical.
Not so much water as law and order.

The word for it might disappear,
the road run through its invisible wall.
The view from here is the border

vanishing around an otter,
swallows, tractor, trailer and damsel-
fly, not so much law as a stretch of water.

Mind your footing on its thin air.
There's the fault whose tremor you feel.
The view from here is a border

gone over and over, a fact of nature,
an impression that's begun to snowball,
not so much water as law and order,

a wavering queue, a detention center,
a dotted line turned block and fractal:
the view from here is the border,
law and order written on water.

On Earth

One-offs, each drop formed about a speck of dust,
fall into the drying greenery of August.
Car doors clunk to, neighbors make their exit.
Summer and there's time to visit.
That time is now.
                        The flowers are an interest
we suddenly wish we'd taken since winter's blessed
the ground with cooler air and a hint of frost.

Summer we're about again to give up for lost,
hot and solitary as we dreamt it.

from Home, Again

Secretarial

The country, sometimes, still appears to ask
    to just be taken down, even by a tourist, on no one's side,
    a tourist lost at home, blue book open, ticking off each task.
But when old Colin, in pajamas, explained how I could evade
    the barbed and electric wire that fenced off fields
    and the bull let loose to scare the stranger off
    (I'd stopped to ask for directions), I was ready to wade
    through cowshit and knee-high grass to see if
the poet, long abroad, was written in the ruin's native life.

Colin stopped me then, leaning on the open door of the Renault—
    noting first the English registration
    I'd parked outside his roadside bungalow,
    and said his father hated that his mother called him Colin,
but he's the one who stuck it out. No one,
    it seems he had to tell me this, no one belonging to them ever had
    to go over to England, a sally he follows up with a question
about where I live, before naming the man on whose land the castle rested:
    we do nothing, he says, but damage what we inherited,

bulldozing the medieval church and causing the collapse
    of the foxhole the settler and his family used, legend has it,
to make, under a smoldering fire, their escape.
    This new heir has his eye on the castle, no doubt.
It will soon be more literature than history. We are not
    all the same, he said. I recall, at the edge of the clearing,
    the grant's nice clause saying the poet had a right
to possess new areas discovered by his survey… To belong,
    a moment's authority is nothing.

The Valley of the Black Pig

The trestle sags, right there
where the pig's big perfect head,
hugely perched on stalky, flat-out forelegs,
unbalances the stretcher.

The stripy-aproned cook
cuts soft fatty meat from its back
onto the paper plates we line up with,
looking it in its char-black eye.

The festival, the feast, is built
around the return,
after years away, of a successful son.
There's a hashtag, a website

and a temporary structure
in the school playground,
a North Kerry weekend
his New World mates signed up for,

going to town
on the hangi details.
The all-age crowd circles
the pit: no Maori stone

in the bog, so they fired metal,
an iron gate, old tractor parts
in a furnace, then put
the lot, iron, coal and all,

into the earth. The chef:
"We wrapped it in wet
jute sacking, with cabbage,
buried it here last night."

The men dig down, hot work
as they strip off their shirts;
a couple of young ones baulk,
covering their mouths

as the animal
in a cloud of heat
emerges from the earth,
arriving among us, its people,

an image
for the front page of the paper,
returned to our language
like a king on his stretcher.

Ruin 2 (Sat Nav Version)

Arriving in the dark, a low satellite gleams
like a high window beyond the orchard.
It has ideas about how things are
and, once in a blue moon, returning,
not sure where I am, things
glitter and twinkle with an underwater look,
every high wall legible as crevice, foxhole,
breathing space, so nothing seems, for an instant,

outside its pale and wholly comprehending mouth,
like the well-bred voice which would correct
every accidental left or right,
until I start to make out, by its light,
the overgrown entrance to the house,
summer retreat turned safe house and symbol.
Hard, escaping the swim of work,
not to fall for its big picture, bumping into

the glassy fact of slow thought
becoming a long life. It lights up
around the sagging, blu-tacked A4 sheet headed
OPW and the sign for visitors
which bars entrance to the tower's kitchen garden
whose apples are dry and sweet.
In the long grass shadows falter where a path breaks in,
flattened stalks unbending, the matted way

dipping every so often to the brown river
no one steps in. It brought us here, the satellite.
It might last forever, a sort of
Anglo-Norman, laying down a route
for which the old map is no help, its flash
visible from the black and watery meadow
that keeps being gone back to, the old names
hovering behind its aspirations.

Colin, Again

"*'Then want I words to speake it fitly forth*':
an idea, a name that will forever be entwined
with whatever crap is written on the counter
or scrawled around the graveyard walls
or scraps of initials and three-hit bands
inscribed on bins by bored and mitching schoolkids.
Who'll write of this as well, when write they do:
it will come into the things they'll dearly name,
fields, animals, the house they marry into and their child,
and that child's children too will know some guise
of this engraved idea I speak of now: POETRY,
the language drawing us out of ourselves,
hollow boon, vacuum, a screen
projecting onto us shades we call our own
which flicker on, as we do and don't intend, redoubled
in a story told across a table or on a walk
among the fields whose stony decorations
we ignore and marvel at alternate days,
even you who hear this song today, rambling off
through acres no one we know has ever owned."
"What has that do with keeping house,
a pint, the match, or who did what to whom?"
"It's the place through which those things can pass,
guttering, into the hard fire we truly see them by.
Someone says I should go and live there, in the fire,
rather than annoying them back here,
but it doesn't work like that, it's what comes and goes."
Now he speaks with what the poet calls "celestial rage."
"I prefer to the stone the river's repetitions
that swim into view like a premonition
which is also déjà vu: we'll remember the Flood
as the waters rise up around our waists,
(the eel and the roach mistaking us for what?).
Over and over a discovered heaven, the first kiss,
the other world that is not all it's cut out to be…"

Swans

The arc of the driveway is what's left,
where someone built a house and tended a lake
to walk beside, discussing politics
and how a tree moves in the wind. Its music
is a jetty drifting away from the boathouse
whose rolled-shut metal door tricks
visitors into thinking it holds a life raft.

The house drifts beyond its purpose,
is demolished for a car park and picnics
and returns in a special room, small, sturdy,
becoming anonymous as its windows empty,
enormous insects swanning around—they own the place—
occasionally stunning themselves on the glass.

On Earth

At the bus stop under the horse chestnut we tally the length of *Boyhood*
against the babysitter's plans for later and, waiting,
see the leaves have started to wilt,
brown at their July edges, losing a little of spring's climb upward;

afterwards, emerged from the dark into a thunderstorm, we see out
the tree's arching welcome to spikes of lightning,
its base flooding,
growing into reduced circumstances, swelling up, but still about.

Is this what it means to be someone? I'm not saying anything,
but twenty-four hours later, the smell in the air is of rain drying off
        stone, *petrichor*,
the tree's slow and seasonal evaporation. A way of answering

to a day, to years of them, that we step into and speak up for.
To you.
There is no one else I am talking to.

Montevideo

after Jules Supervielle

I was being born and at the window,
passing by, was the horse pulling the plow

in from the brightening edge of the far field,
a mosaic which tile by tile the light revealed.

Who was driving it? Whoever was up
woke the day with a little pop of his whip,

night's other element an archipelago afloat
above the day he had started,

walls raising themselves from the sand and cement
and river gravel that had waited in them, sleeping tight.

A little bit of soul, my soul, slipped by,
along a blue rail, a line in the sky,

and another bit folded itself
into a sheet of paper, under sail, adrift,

till it lodged under a stone,
its wildness caught and settled down.

The morning counted its birds,
never losing its place.

That sweet honeysuckle smell
gave itself to the morning's blue swell.

In Ireland, on the Atlantic,
the air was so affable, such a tonic,

that the colors of the horizon
came closer—to see the houses we lived in.

It was me being born, there where the woods almost speak,
on whose paths the grass grows, surely—but not too quick:
underwater, equally, seaweed and algae bob and wave:
the wind too will fall for them, they make believe...

Earth, always about to begin again its orbit,
recognizes us in its atmospheric dips,
feels, in the wave *and* in its profoundest deeps,
the swimmer's head, the diver's feet.

The Penny

I mustn't have sunk it in the water after I found it behind the shed
because here it is, the penny, back again in my pocket,
or it fell out anyway, so getting out of bed
it was there, shiny-eyed, on the carpet.

It's nothing, and don't make it into something,
just a penny, a little coin that wouldn't stick.
Don't make out it's a sign or has a meaning
like a bottle imp or some unquenchable storybook candlestick.

OK but did you see me try to give it away,
a tip for that terrible chowder we stopped for earlier,
by the lake, do you remember?, the day before yesterday,
and it came back staring up at me from the saucer.

I remember and the waiter's looking back at you as if
that were a tip. I'm getting up, I hear someone,
calling. Forget it. This is a holiday *and* there's enough
to worry about without this carry-on.

I'll just leave it right here—no point, is there?,
in doing anything else and, after we've left
then we can see if it's all square,
if it stays here on the counter or if it is something daft;

you'll see, we'll turn around, a mile from the door,
for the camera or a toothbrush or *Battleship*
or a passport the kids made a game for:
if it's gone or makes it home before us will it be got-up

or if it looks up, becoming useless, from the dash as we embark,
what look will you shoot me in the below-decks dark?

The Rebuild

Walking upstairs into the dark—
they'd ripped out the electrics
to put in the new stairs—
she gripped where the banister had been

and tipped a little, as though she'd taken a drink,
or lost a heel, or aged overnight by years,
but steadying herself she went on
making another note of what must be fixed

and entered the plasterboard attic
which emerged from the dark as bins, papers,
a toolbox, a bucket of water with a half pint of milk in,
all half lit by the roof-opening Velux

and the fancier wall-mounted window—black,
argon-filled—which she'd known,
as she signed the check, she'd paid too much for
and knew now (as she stepped around the nails and tacks

that dotted the dust-thick floor)
were doing no good at all, letting in
not only the noise of the last birds flying back
to the garden's rowans and lilacs

whose waving branches she could hear
swaying in the late evening's cool sonics—
familiar, quiet, unpredictable music
above the shattered old roof on the unmown lawn—

but also, farther off, a bus's creaking brakes
at the stop a street away, hearing even,
the torch in her hand, the doors clatter open and the driver
name the price, there and back.

Household

Without disease, the healthful life;
The household of continuance
    —Henry Howard, Earl of Surrey

A bowl of water shakily reflects
the lilac in bud again,
the newly dug bed like a headscarf
small blackbirds dart from
to the sunlit tree,
stringing things along
before night slides in
among green leaves,
knowing no end
to their swaying to and fro,
the bright wind a table
at which I stand, again,
feeling a way into things.

Light dragging
its heels past six o'clock,
you offer, out the back door,
"First spring walk in the park?"
on your way,
knowing what I'm like.
Though the first wasp
flies straight back, for good,
into a hole in the wall
you're already stood at the cross,
making a cloud. The moon,
pitched low and thin, issuing
like steam from tea.
The trees, barely in leaf,
meet in shadows
on the finally shining roofs.

Before I say a word,
"Don't start," you say. This
is unfinished spring,
close to the edge of things,
watch it, half green,
half petal-strewn, the lilac
budding penny-brown.
Our faces, look,
peer from the house's
black mirror at our first return.

It's not, is it?, as if this
never happened before,
the wind gusting
where the trees bud, the gate
shutting at later dusks
till parents shout
children's names
because it's time to go:
where the rain patters now
(I'm all for settling down
inside at last)
sand will glitter
on tarmac footpaths
cutting across inexplicable fields.

Astronaut

Sawing in half the cast-iron bath he says the house was built around
so that he can ship it, in parts, downstairs and out to the skip they've
    hired,
Neil, who is putting in the new electric shower, says to her, "The heating's
gone off now and the water too, but I'll come back later." Climbing, *much*
    later, into bed
after her night on call in the freezing north, she starts to ask him, her
    husband, if Neil did,
return, that is, from wherever it was he went with the bath in pieces,

when she finds he is dead to the world with herself beside him, so begins
the careful, gravityless stepping around of an astronaut,
discovering on the bedside table, between "how-to" books and the baby's
    bottle, the thermostat
he must have fallen asleep trying to reset, the temperature setting, as
    the unfolded booklet says,
unknown but, read by the alarm's red glimmer, closer to the second of its
    two settings,
not the one called "Sun (or Comfort)," but "Moon" which, it says,
    could be described as "Off."

A noise, in the pipes, the other side of the wall, where the old bath was,
that she ignores, along with the distractions of the rain and the state of
    the discarded floor,
a sea of disappointment it is as impossible to float away from as it is
to understand, in this light, at this hour, the word "Commissioning,"
or performing the "Initial power up" or asking, by the light of her phone,
    how to set the timer,
when it is too late to set the clock, everyone is leaving,

the door is shutting behind her like the set sun, and the idea of "comfort,"
as she exits a week of nights for a week of nights, is not what anyone
is after in the shortening days they are aimed for…
Within one minute the old set values—she is turning in her sleep now—
    must be checked.
And there is no one to whom this can be reported. The equipment,
what's left of it, will persist. From now on, as before, she is on her own.

Downstairs, next morning, the house is warm, they're all out of bed.
He's put the thermostat in the fridge and boiled the last of the water
    with milk
for a restoring coffee: the big two are in their uniforms and ready for
    road;
by the skip in the drive he stands with the buggy, scarfed and gloved,
taking in instructions for the day ahead—what to say to Neil, we need
    milk,
what needs taking out of the freezer, when to call, all my love.

from Knight

for Róisín, Ronan and Clíona

warlike arms, the idle instruments of sleeping praise,
were hong upon a tree
                    —*Spenser*

1. Sword

He marches into the yard and calls all comers
in a flurry of blue and silver: he slips; he recovers;
he is the monsters he describes; roaring, he blinds
each foe, then mortifies or turns his enemies to stone; he finds,
in special cases, a new power, transmuting stone to dust
or, whirling anticlockwise, kills, with a spell, what moves too fast.
He lays out his charms and conquests in the porch,
a captive doll, a sheaf of horsetails, an old stopped watch,
then, saying nothing, presents to me his lightsaber,
the blue tubing scuffed from the action, the handle's silver
not so worn I can't make out its outlined lightning bolt.
When I ask about the mess it's made he says it's no one's fault,
retracts the blue point so it looks like a relay baton
and, coming closer, makes as if to pass it on.

2. Shield

His shield he made himself, out of an old Amazon box,
having taken a kitchen knife to saw a heart shape out,
its edges rough, piped, serrated. He unrolled tinfoil and tore,
papering the board with it and, from the sewing box, he took
two strips of red felt and fixed a cross to the shining foil.
Ready, after this ordeal of composition, craft and toil,
he made his way into the green yard and charged
but met, he could not believe his luck, the long broad axe

of the magnolia's lower bough, where the shield still hangs,
because as he pulled it back it seemed to snag
and lodged there further. Retelling the story
after he had been disturbed—someone calling
as he dealt out busy pain—he said he drew his wand
and made the green scene a whited-out pond, a sepulcher,
forgetting that yesterday he'd told us all the wand was no more,
destroyed as he took issue with a neighbor in the rain
and that, as he spoke, it was easy to see over his shoulder,
the red and silver shield shining, in the sunset, from the tree.

At a Concert

He reaches for a scrap of paper as the crowd files in,
fumbling it out of an overcoat beneath the flip-up seat.
The quartet, in their appointed places, tune up: he keeps
to himself the feeling this might be the part

he will enjoy the most. Tall, rumpled, all in black,
the composer is the image of a curate who kept him behind,
in the sacristy, one morning to count collection money.
The arresting opening bar strikes home and he feels

not at all bad, singled out even, though he worries
as the counterpoint continues, if that pain
coming into focus in his right eye is a scratch, he hopes not,
or a sty, which would be painful—he turns off his phone—

given the week he has ahead, the flights, there and back,
seeing his family, long journeys he'd like to read through.
But the half-stripped hallway and dented car, he arches his neck,
are on his mind and he wishes this passage would end

as he notices the light seeming to shift behind the cellist
gathered around her instrument like a slept-in coat,
and a familiar color shines in the half-lit front row
which he forgets, responding to the cellist's

sudden frenzied relieving response to the violins' permutations.
In Niagara once, by himself, he photographed the spray
and a boat that circled and almost tipped over, knowing
behind him stood gewgaw stalls from which he'd take something away,

thinking of this, as the applause starts, unprepared, eyes abrim,
someone had said, yes, there would be no interval,
so this was it, over before he was ready, and around him,
in the rustling coats, the shifting sounds of conversation.

Snail Days

Back and forth to town and ocean:
the train that takes us, snail days,
runs between like a thought,

a thought with rain streaking it
and fields like a faithful companion.
A swaying to which we listen,

coming, here and there, to terms
with the tide's systemic pulse,
the Atlantic silver like a city at night.

An Briathar Saor

Having cleared almost everything
we miss the piano and the bicycle on our return.
The piano went north, in a horsebox.
Not an ornament or even a photo is left
in the space where the sideboard has been.
The bed frames and mattresses are gone
from the bedroom where we ask
about the bike. A wheel will go east,
it's said, a pedal south, the chain west.
One story slopes away from another,
brother and sister, mother, father.
Put them together, you'll get the picture.

House at Night

Because there's no one else around
you like the house at night.
Silent phones, a blank screen,
cherry blossom edging
the extra hour. Nothing to do.
No one's going to call.

                        Spring,
a forgotten pocket you dip into,
turns up a late ray of light
across your mouth
and neck.
House at night, last
a little longer!

To the Management   (2019)

after Horace, Epistle *1.14*

for Roy Gibson and David Matthews

Manager of my offices and working week,
could we figure out, statistically, which of us does better?
You, grounding strategy in bricks and mortar, or me
tightening the screw on a phrase or an image. Let's try and see
which is the better commanded, my field or yours.

I call that poet lucky who writes at a kitchen table,
following a line, leaning into its every tautening. You call
blessed the one who has gotten away. But your *dullsville*
I walk around like a lord: on tree-lined dusty side roads
the goldfinches' arrival or a tide of copper leaves
can tempt me into detours. And when I arrive,
never late, at my local, there's a friendly face,
Ceefax in one corner on a small screen and no "next
big thing" in the offing. (Envying another
is to hate your own place, and know no other.)

When you lived in the capital, slavishly filling in forms,
analyzing data for reports, you dreamed
of going home to the provinces with new knowledge.
Now you long for bright lights, a famous face
made out on the underground. Stuck here, you cut
and paste the formal requirements, doing
what you're told. This is your life, to wear
a suit that won't be outshone by the accountants,
(and yes I like the cut of those unstructured, wide-leg outfits),
to discover figures that will survive an audit, to pluck outcomes
from colleagues who hadn't planned for them, who resist
every innovation, and whose wisdom is to wait
on five-year cycles and a change of minister. Money,

money, money. What you are proud of, I can see:
the shining hair, toned body and those specs (which start
to look a little dated now, like everything futuristic)
that got you into the capital's clubs.
Famous night schools and a society you'd only heard of
are fondly "recalled" over flat whites
at whichever chain just rented the corner site
at our campus's dead margin. But
such foolishness is OK over a simple meal. I know.

When I robe up and read out the students' names
at the end-of-year ceremony, doffing my silly hat
and mispronouncing every other unusually accented name
my neighbors laugh. There, but for the grace of God. I join in
while you are looking at your watch, measuring out
small talk, cursing fate, the latest message putting you on edge,
dreaming more and more of the Royal Mile.

It is half accident and some design, the easy life I live,
and will always return to, tanned, as you will see,
and with a taste for the fine balance of Occitan reds. I did,
once, think I'd fit in around the oval tables you sit at,
poring over figures, filtering, recombining…
But this dumb ox, making lines in his narrow field,
would not be happy to have, best outcome, his head turned
by some stranger from the court decreeing
"What a fox!"
                    Awkward as the fit might be,
and knowing where these lines are going—
I can say "nowhere" as quick as anyone!—
I stand over their numbering days, searching for occasion
in every leaf that falls to earth.

THE KABUL OLYMPICS (2020)

The Axe

Around us, this one of many houses' slow, broadening
expansion into ideas about love, bushes emerging as a border,
the drive's uneven, herringbone undulation of stone
fostering greenly weedy outcrops. The rose—
a neighbor's—sprawling; bins growing smaller and more various,
a new window not designed as a moon box. But which is.
The window admits the moon and the axe waits

for the conifers which cast fat shadows on the walls
and rise into the clouds whose indiscipline I love.
The drone and rumble of traffic swims in and past;
in its wake regulations, differently colored lines,
notices we mean to recycle, matter-of-fact accruals
to be taken out under the discriminating trees which grow,
year on year, across the growth forecasts

you and I sit out, part of a big picture
which hangs on a word. Here is the strong trunk
and branch of our nights and years,
and the obscure hours which greenly filter light
and baffle sound; what hangs over us,
and these subsiding houses, started with a question
finding the ear of another, making its impossible offer.

Germany

You feel free on its motorways
at night, *caution*
another language as you slip
endless summer roadworks,

new words draped over
signposted place names and numbers
you'd anyway found hard to trust.
Oh, this driving into the dark!

Shift the full beams to dips
until—pushing when you ought
to pull—they go out
and you rocket into

a silence where no one
knows what you are.
Black Hanoverian nights
in the heart of July! And

on the other side of this
almost silent vacuum,
wait, unbelievably,
eight days of hating

rye bread, Hefeweizen, borscht,
hot nights ending
on a sofa bed wedged against
a pointless radiator...

But now, wheel-spinning through
black German forest, cities
a rumor you will not snatch at,
is to be content for once,

all in, completely alone
and certain as an engine,
going for the exit, full tilt
among the folksongs.

A Minute to the Hour

The lilies open in the darkening front garden, the rich, dense scent
    reaching into
the drive and porch, and out the footpath to the turning circle

I criss-cross, reversing nightwards between brown and green bins
into what is not so much crisis as subsidence with just the greenery
    welling up.

In the back, grapes and tomatoes blush and fatten, and smoke
from the neighbors' rises across the fence. The heat thickens; disorders

surface like insects crawled out from the cracks where weeds star and
    dust the stone.
A red moon, as forecast, tilts faces upward. A hawk descends,

taking the blackbird, and with it the idea of speed without purpose,
acceleration as an end in itself. Fumes rising into the biosphere. Coughs

and allergies are out in the open; every step is measured and
    accounted for,
our lives transparent. The earth furrowed, layered,

and us looking at hybrid cars. The children slumber through the
    afternoons,
dreaming of days spent with cousins who are patient and hopeful.
    Nocturnal

and wild, sparring, out of sorts, it has taken ours all night to settle down.
Live in the moment is what the daily paper advises, but here is a long view:

go around the house after turning off the downstairs lights and
     checking the doors;
walk into one room after another, call out the names

like a god whose time is not yet gone. Open
a window to pull in a last bit of scent off the climbing jasmine;

low clouds thicken, not so far away, where the action is said to be
     taking place,
the moon at the mercy of Mars, this minute of the larger hour.

Ledwidge in Manchester

Having made mincemeat of his shoulder he convalesces,
not knowing, but—really—*knowing* that some Father
will sooner rather than later record he was blown to pieces
stopping in out of the drumming rain for a cuppa

with his unit... In Ypres. A different unit
from the one he has left in the Balkans for the upset assembly
around him in Lily Lane, in a schoolroom they've had to refit
as a men's ward, so national is the level of casualty.

This is in the run-up to Easter, April 1916.
What catches his attention in the tightening plot is new daffodils
bending under the northwest wind. It's been and gone.
The not much that lies ahead of him, and helpless symbols.

City of Trees

22 May 2017

Their greenness is a kind of grief.
                    —*Larkin*

I would give Manchester back to the shepherds...
                    —*Wilde*

At the Town Hall valedictory do the curator's art in parks—
her metal tree—and the gallery's diversity get credit
which she abjures: "Luck is the residue of design,"
a quote which, around the room, sparks
applause, not for herself, or the line,
nor of course the fact that she is heading south,
but that it asks for this new order to be acknowledged,
and sees the city's sprawl as *managed*.

Cycling back, under the candled chestnuts, past the gallery
and through the Curry Mile's neon influence—
its last two Irish pubs, the Clarence
and the Whitworth refitted now as a Christian café
and a chrome-and-glass shisha bar—the crowd
is nothing on the night twenty thousand Libyans gathered
at the southern end, celebrating the death of Gaddafi,
hours after it was announced on the BBC

whose old beehive building they'd camped beside, in protests,
for months. Fireworks, flags, biscuit-tin drums and gunshots,
a party for the ages, like that afternoon on the allotment
digging in the spuds when the neighborly
encore of cheers rolled in, Agüero*oooo* going global
on the end of Balotelli's flick. City,
going wild, submerging in its element
those who'd once thought otherwise. Mental.

133

By the time I got home the news had pictures:
a roadblock, ambulances and squad cars
pulled up outside the Arena. Overnight, it was first
numbers, then names, and the Council Leader
on the Town Hall steps, in the same shirt
I'd seen him in twelve hours earlier,
and the mayor taking the microphone
to promise "business as usual," a not exactly steely line

he would repeat; likewise, "The city will not be divided,"
and "goes from strength to strength." A man
is arrested outside the Morrisons in Chorlton,
a door is blown in in Fallowfield.
Where the Libo Cargo van would park
white police trucks mark the corners.
At a concert I dismantle the book bag I've lugged from work
while the metal detector queue slows and meanders.

The summer nights demand updates; we write
to friends about our kids, the schools
stay open as they "process" classmates'
tales of sleeping in a hotel overnight;
the footage of a man with luggage on wheels
buying bits and pieces in a corner shop circulates,
this watchful ex-student, born here, ill at ease,
walking through the May weeks of the trees'

slow green explosions, the air
thick with willow pollen and honeysuckle,
all invisible in the greyscale's pixel
rendering of the place, scrambling it
even as crowds gather elsewhere,
in shops and bars and streets, to shoot the breeze,
watch a match on telly, and follow their phones,
as I do, student of uprootings and aftermath,

hemmed in by the information
which descends on us like summer rain,
the stories and images as much a distraction
as each attempt to make it all align,
the sequence getting out of order
which would track us as we move on from the rooms
and fields and trees of the city's hundred towns
whose separating griefs harden and endure.

The Kabul Olympics

i.m. Caroline Chisholm

She decided on swimming the Channel
to think through the chances
of a character escaping the camps in Calais.

When the weather turned the organizer
had to cancel, but training in the murky Dover water
was not all beside the point:

Swimming Pool Hill
would be the name of the novel.
The hill was where a swimming pool had been,

built by a Russian
dreaming up an Olympics in Kabul,
before the rise of the Taliban.

She lived with story. She added one word
to another, to make more probable
what ought to happen.

The unfinished novels were visitations,
chances we should take. While she wrote
we listened, friends

piling now out of the slow black car.
When the weather turned
she knew what it meant.

She had terrible luck is what she wouldn't say.
Her laughter started at
the back of her throat

and tilted her head. She'd call up,
after writing her character
into the Channel;

chances were she couldn't tell
from day to day
where she'd be living herself.

Younger, she rode off on a horse, it was a white horse,
seen from an orchard: her amazed father,
diminishing on the border,

is unforthcoming on the details.
They didn't matter, this isn't a story.
That noise is probably the wind.

They drained the swimming pool at the top of the hill,
a quiet spot, to test for innocence.
She could hear its dry echo.

Something unspoken can be something known.
Saying it
would be another desperate matter.

St. Patrick's Day

At the embassy launch, silver service for forty, I'm enjoying the lamb
I've given up for Lent at home
as a way of making the children (and us)
think about the choices they might make, choices

I make small talk about with my neighbor, who represents Irish
        impressionists,
hazy watercolors in blue and grey and green
for which, she explains, a market exists.
A PR looks up briefly from her phone

and confidingly discloses, a look over either shoulder, what she inherited.
Doing the rounds, the minister glazes over
until someone mentions her constituent,
here for work as well, cooking in the kitchen. She brightens when he is
        summoned upstairs,

while we stand, the guests, with the lamb forgotten, to shake her
by the hand, running through the pitches we've practiced and repeated
to each other. A stadium, a circuit,
an archive. Sometimes, in outdoorsy weather,

I am cycling to work and *know* I've dropped or somewhere lost the,
where is it, hi-vis vest I suddenly see
when I look down
I'm wearing all the time. It's fine,

like the drink I find in my hand
that I'd left, I thought,
on the ante-room table and which, before the toast is proposed, I need.
The table, a historian said, as we moved away from it,

was the Liberator's, now an emblem we place our drinks on,
or don't, as the small talk takes a turn
to the voter in the kitchen,
and our travels, from all over, to this corner of London,

my blue morning spent, across town, in an artist's studio,
    a converted chapel,
roof replaced with glass,
the interior's cold spring brightness amazing, natural,
stepladders leaning on veiled walls,

the source of it all
the pictures of cloudy white and the darker greens
I sat under, making notes at a long wheeled table
we had tea on, with the scones

and jam an Iranian collector
had deposited as a gift. (Years ago, in the capital on a visit,
a weekend away, together, unable as usual to find a place there to eat
that looked good and wouldn't cost the earth

we settled on falafels from a street cart
and in the photograph you took that night
the flash whites out the detail of the figure I cut,
just anyone on a street, but knowing where to turn, to the light.

Which pours, hi-vis, blinding element,
into the room.) Now we are asked to raise our glasses. What for?
The minister, as she must, moving on to the next engagement,
and the ambassador,

a handshake and smiles for the histories
and memoirs he passes through, spelling this out: our friends
dotted around this city are unvisited, in private houses,
whose days also meet their ends;

the blank page under a blue sky blackens
what we cannot see into lines,
like something the waiting birds can land on
and call from, looking askance

at the glasses of light adrift on the tablecloths,
empty as the lobby chit-chat
for which there will soon be other mouthpieces.
Over there—can anyone believe it?—is the palace.

The Places

But she is miles away, the laptop's elbow in front of her,
the phone squirrelled into her pocket still peeping out,
the places I call her from as distant
as the town to whose blue mood I return, every year,

with its special combinations of cloud: on the line are delicates
the rain is on the point of coming for, the river below
rising and no through road. *Back up…* This picture defaults
to a room which is not all there. Partial, screened, it is hum and glow

and pings. *Tired? Hungry?* Evening's subjunctive moods
color questions and commands, *either* and *or*
descending from kitchen and sofa into the old woods
our vanishings are lost on. The bare lawn and sudsy river.

Will we go? Remember parking the car on the pier.
The kettle, the moon. *Come on.* This *will still be here.*

Two Vases

I.

Belleek. Chipped, for the first time,
on one of our moves (London? Here?), now broken—
whoever tried moving it, or by whatever tremor shaken,
and suddenly communicating

                                  a big noise and the inside
turned out and lit as it had never been,
its white narrow interior and what it held,
the water—a film on the counter
         reflecting light onto the ceiling,
and flowers, pinks, roses, the green
            tangles they came from and, remember,
            lilies which smell off
                and stayed in their cellophane wrap.

The split vase
            and spilt water—flowers it has seen,
hands that moved it, the tables set
that it set off, the dressers and sideboards
traveled between, thirteen years
under the same roof, and the flowers
because we want color and the rooms' dust and absences
are forcefields that asked, out of hours, for color
and a well
            to sink them in,

now mosaic, the porcelain the flowers dried out in
which was more than
                ornamental
releasing scented head-turning clouds.

2.

The pieces swept up and set aside until,
back at my clutter of desk, book and screen,
I look up at,
      having forgotten it,
                its twin,
the other, identical vase
we received that same wedding day,
creamy, iridescent curves and scribbles of green dotted shamrock,
its "flowery tale" high above the room on the Welsh dresser,
landed among mixers and two finished wooden models,
   one a precariously balanced sailing ship,
     the other a rooster,
this remaining vase coolly at home up there where it had been forgotten,
a drink of air in its open mouth.

A Lifted Bridge

February

The Council closed the road and hauled the railway bridge,
on a lorry, to a corner of Fog Lane Park,
where I lap it, unable to get enough of its missing ends,
its suddenly taking no one anywhere. February,
prickly, raw, encourages resolution
and I am still running, weeks later,
around grass flattened when the bridge was landed.
Then it's gone, and the grass has been dug up,
and a cherrypicker and JCBs are parked in its stead.

March

The new grass is sown. Magpies and gulls
peck at the absent brown where the bridge's
weight-bearing shadow fell. Mud and water
still fenced off like an overflow car park. Up the road,
newly supported and a few feet higher, the bridge
bears shuttles and high-speed London trains
through March's low east winds, maybe seeing the top
of the snowdrop-haunted, bluebell-swimming wood
the dog, following his nose, does his best to get lost in.

April

Now light changes around the last runner,
drawn back by milder weather, and the last dogs
follow owners out the clanging gate,
the park an empty space fog descends into and into
the indents where the bridge was and the western end
where the lemony sun has set. There is
a wateriness around the greening spires brimming
into the dotted night, which I will go back to—
however we get from there to here—come what may.

The Harbors

1. The Manifest

The bankrupt travel agent bought them the *Eksund*,
and took a cut. He said

he was to hand over £700,000 in plastic bags and, more personal,
a double bed, a large clock, olive oil

and a German Shepherd flown from Frankfurt
to Valletta, the boat's last recorded port.

The sea was too rocky
so they docked and loaded at the military harbor in Tripoli.

Spotted departing, observed daily from the air, tailed, surrounded,
the engineer wanted it to go down like lead,

to scuttle the boat off the Breton coast,
but misfired the one faulty timer in a "breath-taking manifest"

which the authorities
would piece together in unbombed cities:

a million rounds of ammunition, guns,
missiles to beat the band and two tons

of odorless Semtex
instead of its advertised cargo of grain. The mooted attacks,

a "*Tet*" offensive,
went west, like an empty boat drifting between wave and wave.

2. The Tempest

And 'twixt the green sea and the azured vault
Set roaring war

The Nimrod recon plane
was not the first sign.
That was a stranger fishing off the end of the pier in Fenit,
in a storm, at midnight.

The *Valhalla*, their contact,
was supposedly swordfish-fishing, in the disturbed seas
off Porcupine Bank.
A long way from the island. So the boys

broke the silence of the water
to mull over what brought them so far offshore,
struggling for cover.
One was recruited, remember,

on the day he buried his father.
Another had a story
of Free Staters dragging a man behind a lorry
through the streets of Kerry.

(My father, less easily led, his one voyage
a warning—a daytrip with a colleague—
which a gale blew into the Atlantic.
Laid low, he fastened himself to the deck.)

In a storm you're out in the open but can't tell
who's your friend,
and their radar, as they moved west, didn't "see" a naval vessel
wearing the Skelligs as background.

When they met the Americans, finally, and ran a long, almost
    extra-territorial line,
and a winch to punt across the crates,
there came the last sign:
everywhere, lights.

One of the boarding party slipped and was "plunged
in the foaming brine," who would have drowned
had they (I hang on to this), not following any order,
not jumped in and saved this undrowned soldier

who they remember as nervous and whose Uzi, a minute earlier,
had squeezed off a few rounds
above their heads.
They would laugh about that later,

seeing dry deaths ahead after years stied
in one part only of the island…
Facedown on the stern then, and punches, rifle butts,
tied in knots.

The sea near the harbor went black and blue
in the blistering southwesterlies. The guns, stacked like rakes,
stood uselessly upright below;
they got stuck into a rebel song, which this storm soaks:

    The runner, the traitor, the Yankee and me,
    the gunner and a spy,
    were wanting adventure and fate,
    none of us cared for the "State:"
    it had a cell with a key,
    and would shout to a sailor, Come with me!

3. The Coast of Nowhere

What and where is meant
by that? An outside,
after-the-fact feeling?
As if the whole show
is over, or as if the old,
much-traveled motor,
almost out of petrol
and miles from any harbor
a traveler would return to,
becomes a stalling delay,
a proper state,

and as when, after
you've finished,
really finished,
sharpening a pencil
the thin wood spirals
off the graphite point,
the graphic point,
its marked-off track
a wavy line, bound
to a diminishing stub,
to which you'll append
this. This. To be
here and nowhere at all.

4. Libya

from Aeneid, Book I 199–206, 207–228

1.

The heat and noise of gatherings outside, then lightning—
like violence breaking through a rabble, boys and men,
stones and worse fired into the air
                                        and where's
the swaying voice whose speech and veteran record
they know and trust? Who can calm them and advise
that there will be another day into which he'll walk with them?
What will suffice to make them listen and stop?

2.

Just then the sea straightened out into a mirror
as its maker turned and oversaw
their route to land under blue and clearing sky:
Aeneas and his crew were set for Libya,
a haven, a breakwater where the swells subside,
drawing ships into a curving inlet,
rugged sandstone pocked by the Ghibli
narrowing to a quiet grotto, above which, a miracle,
leafy fringes of pine, juniper, cypress, olive,
the outer edge of a coastal oasis
joined to the caves by a freshwater spring
which ladders the living rock. This is the place
whose natural, shelving ledges the wood nymphs love,
where, anchor weighed, ships come to rest,
and weary sailors lift their hands and praise the gods.

Green

There's the flag. Now,
have you a line?
Don't look up. Head
down. Pine cone, broom,
the tee, the rough, wind,
the grip, the lesson,
Cliff House, no one's beach,
Nuns' Beach,
Loop Head, concentrate,
or it could go anywhere,
Titleist, the pockmarked moon,
The Bunker, the *Leithreas*,
the seaweed bath, the transmitter,
the Hotel, asylum-seekers,
the castle, the slots, lost
and not to be found,
the *Tinteán*, the house built on sand,
and closer to the tee,
remember the line,
the graveyard; forget
the westerlies,
the playground, the pool,
presidential bronze, grooved steel,
the straight long undulating road,
America level, God above.
The Atlantic, the Atlantic,
and the verge where I live,
planting my feet squarely.
Now, swing.
Follow through.

Try again.

Confessional

This private thing was owned by all.
                                        —Allen Tate

Somewhere else it might have been perfect for birdwatching
or writing a novel, or repairing small machines.
It faced across the lawn to the drive and front door,
each neighborly call visible
from where I had stowed away, the old confession box,
which, now that I remember it, shrinks,

the lawn sloping towards this not-quite shed,
something like a wardrobe, with two wicker flanks,
an arch where the central door should have been, and inside,
where you might expect more space,
a narrow chamber and solid timber floor,
too awkwardly shaped and small for the lawnmower.

Ported in from a convent by the last owner,
a kind of gazebo, a curiosity, home to a rake and hose,
childish things, a flat ball, and plastic, terracotta-colored
plant pots gathering dirt and, at that time,
cigarette butts and burnt matches.
A place to hide, and to look out from,

the river whispering behind its back and birds rising up
into the lilac from the lawn around it, and then above and beyond
the town's crossroads and square... This bare interior,
the blue and white paint peeling from the wicker,
a basket-weave, criss-crossing the sound of the river
which broadens under the concrete bridge, the salmon

escaping the drag nets and cages. And this wooden box
painted blue and white and hedges adjoined to it,
a sheltered, upright spot, is a place I go to,
a small vault with an echo
of the acts of contrition and miniature blessings
where the salt Atlantic wind bent trees

into a row, *rrrrrrrr*, around ruins. These are places
where the robin and the crow and the seagull must cohabit.
Own up to that, writing down
other answers
to the questions that were handed on. The river
is a temptation whose rough rhythms

no boat negotiates, where we drown the bodies
of the voices our words come from. It is a duet,
two silences, here and nowhere else.
An invisible orchestra waits
and a mermaid conductor you can't see
who twists and smooths these shapes and shadow boxes.

Cold War

A day of days: I roll myself into the sandy dune,
hiding from where the others have gone,
on my own, with paper and pencil,
a towel and book and water bottle.
This is perfect. I hear every whisper,
I know what the reeds report and see the tickle
and hiss of the sandflies. I spear
my thigh with a snapped-off bulrush, and peer
at where the skin raises a bubble. I turn over
and on the flat of my back inspect
the sky for Russian planes. What did it mean,
when we left the mobile home, for my mother to say
something I couldn't hear. The way
to the beach forever-slow and silent.
The sand extends its hot dry atmosphere.
What I am sketching is half alien, half insect.
I could run off. I'd heard *something* sinking in. Listen,
no one is coming to check where I've been.

Suit

for Róisín, 23 August 2019

Our eldest likes its cut
and keeps her eye on it,
would take it in at the waist,
a jagged shorter hemline, pleats…

My father's sober suit
has lived upstairs
through half-frozen nights
to which I wore shop-bought suits,

which have returned, dry-cleaned,
unrepaired of tears,
fraying seams, a stain, one time burned
(it was the age of the cigarette),

while his unreplaced outfit,
wide as boards in leg and sleeve,
has ghosted each house move,
the children growing out

of what we meant for them. The extension
might have been built around *it*.
"I could," she says, "always try it on,"
what I call *my suit*.

Clippings

Clippings, following up on the phone call, are the first *news feed*,
clocking updates from all over. Folded pictures,
and snipped column, and wild review are filters;
likewise the enclosing note ending *Love and God Bless*
on pale blue Basildon Bond. And what she means is understood.
Once (I am 9 or 10, acting as if there was no use

in my thinking she's the center of the world),
my mother left the kitchen with tap running
over a half dozen peeled eggs in the steel sink.
The water's a blur. Has she gone up town for milk?
The eggs are white and grey. And then the car returning,
her voice extending into the household.

Or the time she took the measure of the kitchen orchard
which crows and wasps descended on. So fruitful
it could not be walked into, and grew worse:
she had it razed and blackly charred.
A rough patch, it travels through other summers
which collect: five French oaks, sessile,

settled in and doing fine; from Caherdaniel,
her mother's montbretia; pine trees that grow
from pine cones ferried back from Bordeaux,
resinous, gummy, in whose shadow survive
a robin, starlings, or is it swifts from the eaves,
and a *spectacle* of grandchildren running in a circle.

These cuttings are raised to prosper; they bend
from the house the empty wind,
know the stars and love the sun;
they have settled in, but look up and summon
with sure, elegant lines (here live a couple
of swells)… She is with me at the kitchen table,

between the fridge and the front door:
both sea and salt, error and adventure,
with the kettle on, or good wine. Here too are postcards
which turn one hundred other kinds of blue. Around
the corner's a suntrap and that American maple
whose season, now that I see it, is a miracle.

Horace, Naming the Days

after Horace, Ode 3.8

The 31st, and I'm at liberty, almost idle,
paid in full and logged off, sending smoke
across the real, burning for connections—
Call over,

I was thinking, my learned friend,
and here you are: let's offer
something up, to living well and days
on which the axe won't fall.

Spring's begun again with sunlight on hail,
brightness surfacing
and extending into night.
This Sangiovese

has had time to breathe so, if you love me,
raise your glass,
to the lights we live by
and their long finish. The vote

is a disaster, you're right,
and likewise this city, the country,
even love and books,
the starry realms shining above us

with glorious has-beens, secret sharers,
informants, dealers, priests
and their satellites
who are planning, soon, but not yet,

another life. Write, *So be it*
of this world. To yourself, as they say,
and nights that, in the foolish light of day,
will not foster regret.

Blown Away

I tried to peg it down, the tent,
with bamboo poles, and hooks, and stones,
and the weight of indoor furniture,
a nest of tables, a primus stove, piled on the interior hem,
but away it flew when the wind came,
catching first on the ash, then off
like a bird spiraling wildly in updrafts,
as if a life that had seemed to claw down on what came
within its grip—the solid ground of love and work—
was not so much gripping as "in the grip of,"
as if each old "I am" and "I do" was useless as the mud floor
when it was engaged athwart, caught up now by something else,
taking its shadow with it, but not this sorry assembly of upright sticks
and empty hooks conjuring (not really) a tethered shape.

The Blackbird

The day's white internal door
opens onto a kitchenful of what's been before:

the kettle steaming up the radio; phone-chirps; clatter
of spoons; fridge hum; the order of things

surviving my wakeful night-time reckonings,
each hour hard to pin down as a handful of water,

each morning, each *year* echoing another I am slow to recognize,
and then, between the pips, *there* is

the air's stillness into which a blackbird submits
the sweetest single high and overlaying sound a minute admits,

rising away as I slope
out of the morning to the end of its ropey, *going* hope,

a creature of its mid-air qualms,
its clustered notes and afterthoughts and *here-I-am*s.

Souterrain (2021)

i.m. Derek Mahon

To wait things out, underground,
laid in with more than a lifetime's treasure;
to settle down with the books and study
what comes along the line.

I understand. This
must be around the turn of a millennium.
Hidden, the mind will return
to a "proper dark"

freed from daylit distraction
to ponder absolutes
and the tenses of its own
cavernous, echoing interiors,

seeing the issue
of the day from an ancient prospect.
But terrors shake
this long night,

the texts losing their place,
soft tissue
between some future and the past perfect,
the pooled floor

rising towards the leaking roof,
which gets thundered over.
Powerful sounds scatter the animals
and the shears rust in an outhouse

while the motorway is lowered
further into the royal hill.
There are other sore spots;
a pilot light

going out at the sun's titanic western edge;
a reddening field
parched by the wind;
myrtle and olive

grow across frivolous libraries,
the flocks gone
to pastures new
who would still graze

on these flattened fields,
their reasonable ground. Imagine
going, knowing that what is buried
promises discovery,

cropping up
like braille for the finger to trace,
making out the pattern
by when it comes to a stop.

Acknowledgments

Thanks to Jeff and Alex at Wake Forest for their sensitive, attentive re-arrangement of this book.

Thanks to the journals, newspapers, festivals, radio programs and podcasts where the work has appeared, especially the *Irish Times*, *Poetry Ireland Review*, Listowel Writers' Week, and Manchester Literature Festival.

Thanks to Peter and all at the Gallery Press—for the care they take with the poems, catching what I miss, and for their support over two decades.

Thanks to my colleagues and students at the University of Manchester and its Centre for New Writing.

Thanks to my friends, the first readers of many of these poems, especially August, Barty, Colette, Daisy, Evan, Fionnuala, Ian, Ian, Jeff, Michael, Michael, Peter, Tom, and Vona.

Thanks to Nancy Long, for giving me the big picture, and thanks to Róisín, Ronan, and Clíona McAuliffe, our excellent company.